Crystal and Reiki
Chak

Discover How to Heal Your Body, Increase Spiritual Energy and Balance Your Chakras with the Power of Crystals and Reiki

Rachel Forest

Table of Contents

The information in the following pages is broadly considered a truthful and accurate account of facts and as such, any inattention, use, or misuse of the information in question by the reader will render any resulting actions solely under their purview.

There are no scenarios in which the publisher or the original author of this work can be in any fashion deemed liable for any hardship or damages that may befall them after undertaking information described herein.

Additionally, the information in the following pages is intended only for informational purposes and should thus be thought of as universal.

As befitting its nature, it is presented without assurance regarding its prolonged validity or interim quality.

Trademarks that are mentioned are done without written consent and can in no way be considered an endorsement from the trademark holder.

Introduction

Congratulations for downloading *Crystal and Reiki for The Seven Chakras: Discover How to Heal Your Body, Increase Spiritual Energy and Balance Your Chakras with the Power of Crystals and Reiki* and thank you for doing so.

From the moment you first decided that you wanted to learn more about crystals, your life has taken a drastic turn for the better. Learning about crystals and how to heal the body, mind, and soul can be a life-changing experience and you've already taken a big step on your life path by simply showing interest.

For whatever reason that you decided to obtain this knowledge already shows that you have a strong sense of faith and belief, this is exactly what one needs to be able to achieve and heal with crystals. There are no special talents or abilities required when it comes to healing with crystals, absolutely anyone can do it. But for many, are not able to achieve their goals and dreams because they lack faith.

Before deciding whether crystal healing works on not, make sure you put all of your beliefs into it. With the correct intentions, crystals, and mindset, you will be able to achieve your goals, whatever they might be!

You will also learn how to open each chakra with Reiki, perform self-healing on yourself, master distance healing, and how to send Reiki to a specific event because when it comes to Reiki, time and distance do not matter! Healing the body, mind, and spirit has never been easier

There are plenty of books on this subject on the market, thanks again for choosing this one! Every effort was made to ensure it is full of as much useful information as possible, please enjoy!

Chapter 1: Crystal Healing for The Root Chakra

The first chakra point is the root chakra, also known as Muladhara which comes from the word "mula" meaning root and "dhara" meaning base or support. The color this chakra is connected to is red which represents energy, power, passion, and love. Specific foods such as any red foods like tomatoes, strawberries, and red peppers, can help open the first chakra. Specific exercises such as running or hiking in nature or doing yoga can also help open the root chakra. Walking barefoot can make you connect to the universe more on a spiritual level, and it can also help one feel more grounded. Meditation, especially with crystals, is known to be the most effective way to open any chakra point. The root chakra provides the feelings of safety, groundedness, and emotional security when it comes to a person's everyday life. This chakra is located in your tailbone or also referred to as the lower abdomen.

A balanced root chakra will provide one freedom from the feelings of anxiety and stress. You feel at peace with your day to day duties and you do not worry if you will be able to pay the next bill, you trust yourself to not stress over related matters. Physically, one would have a healthy body with no problems relating to the lower abdomen, plenty of energy to carry on with their day-to-day activities, and the feeling of being safe and secure in life.

Emotionally, a balanced chakra has a well mental balance, no negative thoughts, and a relaxed mindset. This will teach the mind how to react to problems without panicking and stressing. An imbalanced root chakra brings up negative feelings such as stress and anxiety as well as an emotional imbalance. When this chakra is blocked, the energy within the body begins to burn out, always making one feel tired and exhausted both physically and mentally.

Physically, this chakra is responsible for any diseases or problems within one's kidney, feet, spine, nerve system, legs, weight issues, sleep disorders, hemorrhoids, and many other problems. Emotional imbalance relates to feelings of anger, fear, and insecure. One who has an imbalance can't deal with occurring problems without panicking.

Crystals for the root chakra:

Garnet can help heal and clear the root chakra. Crystals such as pyrope, almandine, and red garnet are perfect to heal this chakra. A garnet elixir or essence can also be used during meditation to help promote the healing energies of this chakra. Simply use seven drops of garnet essence about two times a day, you can use once in the morning and once in the evening while taking some time to meditate. Continue using the essence for at least two weeks. Another perfect crystal for the root chakra is a carnelian, specifically a red carnelian. This crystal works by keeping the healing vibrations close to your root chakra in order to keep the healing process going and active throughout the day.

Black tourmaline is another great crystal for healing. Black tourmaline works to heal the root chakra as well as balancing the meridian within one's body that extends from the crown chakra all the way to the root chakra.

Lastly, the tiger eye crystals are used to empower the root chakra and speed up its healing process.

When you first buy your desired crystal or crystals, do not forget to cleanse them first. It is up to you if you want to work with just one crystal or proceed and use all of the above. Having more of the higher vibrational energy within the house will help the body keep its vibrations high too. In fact, after your meditation healing with crystals, make sure you choose a pocket crystal or a bracelet crystal made out of any of the root chakra crystals and carry it with you every day to ensure that the root chakra remains at a high vibration throughout the day, it will make the healing process easier.

Crystal healing for the root chakra:

1) Start off by making sure you are in a secluded area with no distractions. Turn off your phone, and lock your doors so you will not be disturbed. Drink a cup of water before you start the healing session.

2) Make sure you are laying down either on your stomach or on your back, do not forget to place a pillow under your head for utmost comfort. Begin by placing the root chakra crystal of your choosing on your tailbone which is located on the lower abdomen

of your body. If you like, you can place more than one crystal on the lower abdomen. You can also choose to sit up if you feel more comfortable this way but you will need to hold the crystal with your hand so it doesn't fall off, coop up your palm and place the crystal inside before placing it on the chakra point.

3) Begin your meditation by taking some deep breaths, inhale through your nose, and exhale through your mouth. Fall into a pattern of breathing slowly while calming your mind and letting go of any thoughts or worries that you might have. Feel your spirits be lifted up, all your worries are being let go as you feel like you are sinking into the bed or the floor, making you feel more connected and grounded.

4) Try to feel the vibration of the crystal if you can, do not worry if you can't because you will be able to feel it in the future as you meditate and heal yourself more. Visualize the energy from the crystal emerging and entering your body in a bright red light which is the color associated with the root chakra. Visualize your energy restoring to its original state, your tiredness and fatigue simply fading away. Any negativity and toxins within your body are being

diminished by the bright red light as it cleanses and balances your chakra.

5) Meditate for at least fifteen minutes or more if you'd like. You may also consider some meditative music that is made to stimulate the flow of energy within your root chakra. Music is known to increase the vibrations of the crystal. The root chakra is also connected to the sense of smell, meaning that burning incense or the preferred essential oils is another way to enhance the balance and clearing of this chakra. Consider eating root chakra foods such as carrots, beets, potatoes, radishes, parsnips, and onions, as well as exercising to stimulate the energy within the body.

Chapter 2: Crystal Healing for The Sacral Chakra

The second chakra is the sacral chakra, also known as Svadhishana which implies "the place of the self". Considering the root chakra is all about the comfort of survival, this chakra is all about your inner emotions that make up your joy. The sacral is connected to the color orange which means victory, self-respect, honor, creativity, success, and joy.

The sacral chakra is located in your uterus within your lower abdomen. This chakra is responsible for the balance within your emotions. It provides the passion that you feel for your life, and the realization of your purpose in life as well as purifying and releasing toxins within one's body, mind, and spirit.

When balanced, the lower abdomen area within your body experiences no physical problems. Your emotions are in balance, you are able to express yourself and not overreact in certain situations. The energy within the body is balanced, meaning one will never feel exhausted or out of energy.

When imbalanced, the body experiences problems within the kidneys, the reproductive system, and the sexual organs. An imbalance can also cause prostate problems, lower back pain, urinary problems, and gynecological problems. This chakra also represents negative addictions. For one to be healthy, you must be able to recognize and ask yourself whether what you are doing is good for you. Change comes from within. By drawing the energy away from what you find yourself addicted to, you will be able to overcome your bad habits. Emotionally, one would always lash out and become mentally weak with strong negative feelings.

Crystals for the sacral chakra:

Tiger's eye, specifically a golden brown colored crystal, works as a perfect healing stone for the sacral chakra. It can balance you physically, spiritually, and emotionally as well as heal your physical body. It can also be used as an energy stone, to increase one's energy within the body and get rid of exhaustion.

Spessartine garnet can also be used for the sacral chakra, it will stimulate the creativity, inspiration, and sexuality within one's body in order to feel more alive and connected to your life. However, this stone shouldn't be used to much, the energy of the spessartine garnet can be too overwhelming to a low vibrational being, so begin with using at least one or two small spessartine gemstones, preferably in a ring or a bracelet.

Another crystal that can be used for the sacral chakra is the orange carnelian which also works as a healing crystal. It helps clear, balance, and heal this chakra as well as boost one's intuition, energize the body, and activate both the sacral and root chakra.

Crystal healing for the sacral chakra:

1) Begin to get comfortable in a secluded and quiet area, without any distractions. You can lay down or sit up for this healing session. Proceed by closing your eyes and begin your deep breathing.

2) When breathing, make sure you inhale through your nose and hold the breath for at least three seconds before exhaling the breath through the mouth and pulling it for another three seconds. Continue to

breathe like this until you get used to this new pattern and are able to focus on something different while still maintaining the breathing pattern.

3) Begin to visualize the breath entering the body, through your nose, as it expands your lungs. When exhaling, visualize all the air carrying out any toxins, negativity, stress, and worry out of your body.

4) Once you feel at peace with no tensions within your body, reach out and take a crystal of your choosing. Hold the crystal on your lower abdomen if sitting up, or simply place it on the lower abdomen when laying down. Bring your attention to the stone, and focus on feeling the pressure that the stone applies to that area.

5) If you are using any other stones, you can hold them in the palm of your hands if you are laying down, that way you will also be taking in the energy from the crystals and directing the flow of energy through your body and to the sacral area. However, if you are sitting up with your legs crossed, you may place each stone on your knee. It will stimulate the flow of energy. When beginning the healing process,

focus on one stone first, the one that has direct contact with your sacral chakra.

6) Visualize an orange color emerging from the stone, glowing and vibrating at a high frequency. Imagine your sacral chakra reacting to this energy and slightly opening. Let the light fall into your body, through the skin, and into the sacral chakra. Visualize receiving healing as the chakra opens and balances itself. If you have a specific problem at hand, then visualize yourself living a free life without that problem.

7) Move your attention to your palms, where the other crystal or crystals are placed. You can always just choose to place on crystal on one hand but make sure to use the opposite hand when healing the sacral chakra again, in order to balance out the energy flow. It is preferred you use two crystals, for both of the hands. If you have trouble focusing on both of them at the same time, you can focus on one side and then the other.

8) Visualize the crystal glowing a bright and vibrant orange color, let that glow sink into your palms or knees. You will start to feel tingling sensations that

represent the energy of the crystal. Visualize this flow of orange light sink into your palms and travel up your hands, through your heart chakra, then through your solar plexus chakra and finally arriving at the sacral chakra. If the crystals are on your knees, then imagine the energy flowing upwards, through your root chakra and arriving at your sacral chakra. That stimulates the flow of energy within the heart and the solar plexus, it is very beneficial when healing one emotionally.

9) Let the energy travel down to the sacral chakra, healing one physically and emotionally as well as stimulating the flow of creativity, energy, and inspiration. Stay in this sensation for at least an additional ten minutes, just let your body naturally guide the crystal energy and heal any other problems that also are caused by the sacral chakra. Once done, set an intention to seal all the gathered energy within your body so even when you are not performing the healing session, your body is still healing itself.

Chapter 3: Crystal Healing for The Solar Plexus Chakra

The solar plexus chakra is the third main chakra within the body, it is also known as Manipura, which means "resplendent gem" and "lustrous gem". This is the origin of one's self-esteem and self-discipline. It enables you to use your willpower to reach towards your dreams and goals dreams, as well as turning the talk and ideas into actions. It symbolizes the color yellow, meaning lively, active, energetic, hopeful, happy, and smart. The solar plexus is located in the upper abdomen region, usually about a couple of inches above the belly button. The solar plexus is yet another strong emotional related chakra, it primarily focuses on raw emotions that consist of frustration, jealousy, anger, and hatred. This chakra is also somewhat associated with the heart and your ability to fully express your emotions with nothing holding you back.

When balanced, the mind experiences a calm, confident, and cheerful state. Physically, the whole body is healthy due to the solar plexus having control over the entire cellular respiration within the body. The flow of Ki is clear and strong. Emotionally, a balanced solar plexus eases the worries of the mind and releases it from any negativity and mental tiredness. A balanced solar plexus promotes happiness, courage, strength, and motivation.

When imbalanced, the mind is clouded with misjudgment, depression, and doubt. Physically, this chakra is responsible for problems within the nervous system, stomach, muscular system, digestive system, liver, and gallbladder. Emotionally, one suffers from migraines as well as a change in mood and attitude.

Healing this chakra will require a lot of willpower, seeing as you first need to overcome your shyness which is what many people with this blocked chakra are suffering from. In order to overcome that, you need to step outside of your comfort zone in order to achieve success.

Take small steps at a time. One concept that really works is 'fake it until you make it', which means for you to act, confident for example, until you actually become it.

Crystals for the solar plexus chakra:

Labradorite, especially one that is a golden-yellow colored stone, it is also known as a sunstone or bytownite. It is used to enhance one's vitality, assertiveness, and confidence which are emotions that are required to balance the solar plexus chakra.

Peridot is a crystal that is used to cleanse and activate the solar plexus chakra. This crystal can only be used to activate the solar plexus and the heart chakra. When activating other chakras in one session, make sure to remove the peridot from any physical contact while working with the other chakras. Once all have been activated, you may wear a peridot necklace to prevent from any negative energies to influence your healing process.

Citrine is another good healing stone for the solar plexus. This crystal should be yellow or golden in color, it works in opening, cleansing, and activating the solar plexus chakra.

The tiger's eye is probably one of the most powerful solar plexus crystal that is used for healing.

Specifically golden-brown in color, this stone can help the solar chakra function properly as well as creating a well-balanced and empowered body, mind, soul, and environment.

Crystal healing for the solar plexus chakra:

1) The solar plexus is deeply associated with the sun, this is a perfect opportunity to use the sun as guidance when opening one's solar plexus. It is preferably that one sits directly in the sunlight and outside in nature, however, one can also sit on a balcony, terrace, or even indoors, anywhere as long as the sunlight is able to touch your body. Make sure you are not disturbed.

2) Begin by breathing slowly, inhale and exhale. When you inhale through your nose, instead of using your chest and lungs to fill with air, use your stomach. As you inhale, your stomach should expand, filling with air as it detoxifies the negative energy and releases toxins. When you exhale, the negative energy is let go, leaving you feeling refreshed, free, and healthy.

3) If you choose to lay down, you would place all of the crystals that you will be using for the session on your upper abdomen. Make sure you have at least three crystals and place them in the following grid bellow which signifies the solar plexus chakra. The two sides of the triangle should be facing upwards. If you choose to use only one crystal, simply place it on the solar plexus chakra, either sitting up or laying down.

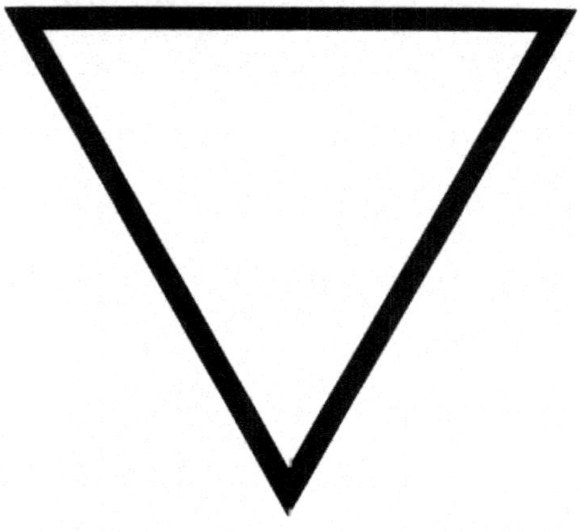

4) Proceed by imagining the energy within the solar plexus emerging in a bright and yellow glow. Let the glow expand before sinking into the solar plexus. Visualize your problems going away, your mind becoming clearer, and knowledge granted for you. If you have a specific trait or problem that you wish to

work on then now is the chance, simply visualize yourself living exactly as you would. Don't let any clouded feelings or worries stop you from visualizing this perfect life.

5) Once the glow sinks in, feel it clear the solar plexus, imagine the negative energy flying out of the body while the positive yellow glow fills you with warmth and happiness. Continue absorbing the energy of the crystals, you will feel some pressure and tingling sensations on your lower abdomen.

6) Continue the healing session for at least fifteen minutes when using one crystal and ten minutes when using three. The formation and the number of crystals work to magnify the energy used, one shouldn't overdo the session otherwise one will have some negative physical effects. However, with the consistency of this session, you will be able to increase the time the more you practice the solar plexus healing.

Chapter 4: Crystal Healing for The Heart Chakra

The fourth chakra is the heart chakra that is also known as Anahata chakra, which means to "unhurt'" This is the origin of one's deep emotions, it represents happiness, kindness, and unconditional love. Your feelings and emotions are all the truth that one is unable to with words. The heart chakra signifies the color green, which symbolizes strength, health, wealth, and success.

The heart chakra is one of the most delicate chakras which is located within the heart area, right in the middle of the chest. This chakra is responsible for love, either receiving love, giving love, or self-love. It is in human nature to be very sensitive when it comes to positive or negative deep emotions or actions, however, with the balance of the heart chakra, this sensitivity will simply fade into the background and one will be able to see the full picture more clearly. The heart chakra works by accepting one for who they are and vibrating at a high frequency with positivity filling the body, mind, soul, and environment.

When balanced, this chakra is able to help when it comes to personal discovery, journey, and development. It also grants peace and comfort in life. Physically, the area in which the heart resigns is healthy and fit such as lungs, breasts, ribs, heart, arms, shoulders and blood circulation. The heart chakra also keeps us alive, although it is very delicate, it is awfully important to continue living. Emotionally, the heart chakra is very vulnerable so when balanced one is able to experience true happiness, and live their life to the fullest by loving and accepting everything that comes in the way.

When imbalanced, the heart chakra experiences negative emotions of hate and negative energy in general, this causes the functions of the body to fail. Physically, this chakra is responsible for the problems within the circulatory system, diaphragm, muscle, immune system, and the respiratory system.

When imbalanced, the body suffers from breast cancer, high blood pressure, lung disease, and many other health issues. Emotionally, this chakra experiences feelings of hatred, jealousy, grief, anxiety, loneliness, isolation, and fear. However, the negative emotions can also affect the physical environment, it can cause separation, emotional abuse, and abandonment.

You can also heal yourself and open your heart chakra through music. Listening to happy music is scientifically proven to lift one's mood up, it can also help open the heart chakra to love. Many people can connect to different songs and music on a more emotional level, releasing tears, anger, or sadness through music can also help move on from those feelings.

Crystals for the heart chakra:

Rose Quartz is the main crystal that is able to balance, cleanse, and open the heart chakra with its strong energy and power of love. This chakra radiates on such a smooth level that it is possible for anyone to feel its vibrations right away.

Apart from healing the heart chakra and giving love to the body, the rose quartz can also give the mind better judgment and clarity when it comes to personal feelings and relationships.

Green aventurine has also a very soothing effect on the body once used to heal. This crystal aims to promote harmony and balance within the body as well as improve any romantic or personal relationships. Peridot, preferably olive or pale green in color, works excellently when it comes to healing the heart chakra. It works to restore balance within the physical body, emotions, and thoughts as well as promoting harmony and better judgment for the future. Period is also used for when one is recovering from a relationship loss of a partner or a friend. Aquamarine can also heal the heart chakra, by cleansing, soothing, and activating the heart chakra. It can also activate the throat chakra which can be used to express the feelings of the heart. However, when using this gemstone, make sure you begin with around five to ten minutes of healing session since this energy is strong which can reveal personal truths that you may not be ready for.

Crystal healing for the heart chakra:

1) When beginning the healing session, try to find a spot when you are exposed to nature. Nature is balanced and peaceful and it is exactly what an imbalanced heart chakra requires. Allow yourself to sit

or lay in nature for a couple of minutes of just breathing deeply and listening to the sounds you hear around you, whether it is birds singing or animal squeaking. Just relax in nature and take in all the energies you feel around you. You will immediately begin to feel at peace.

2) Begin breathing. Imagine the air coming through your nose, detoxifying and circulating in your lungs and chest area before leaving through your mouth. Imagine all the negativity simply leaving as you exhale and let go of any feelings of hurt, betrayal, or fear.

3) Either sitting up or laying down, choose one or more crystals to use to open the heart chakra. Hold them in your palm or set them on your chest, if you choose to set them on your chest, make sure they are not touching each other. You can choose to set them in any layout you seem fit.

4) Begin by visualizing a green bright light radiating from the crystals, allow yourself to breathe deeply and connect to the glow. Relax your chest and let the glowing green glow sink into your heart, opening the

chakra and healing the wounds that the past left on your heart. Feel yourself becoming more open to love with loving energy directed your way from the crystals.

5) Choose one or a couple of people to send loving energy to. Think of that person and visualize sending your love into the universe by simply making a white glow emerge from the heart. As that white glow leaves the body, direct it to your loved one by visualizing the person's face. If it helps you concentrate, say the mantra 'I radiate my love to you' while visualizing their face. Continue this brief exercise for at least one more person.

6) Continue the session for no more than fifteen minutes. End the healing session by thanking the universe for what you already have. You should also consider keeping a gratitude journal, it will help one experience more love and it can help open the heart chakra. When you give love, you receive love.

Chapter 5: Crystal Healing for The Throat Chakra

Vishuddha is your fifth chakra, your throat chakra, which translated to very bright or pure. The throat chakra, the fifth chakra, is located in your throat and neck region. It is responsible for your communication and your expression of what it is you feel and think. Not only that but you are able to inspire yourself and those around you by listening and expressing your own opinions. When imbalanced, one either becomes shy or talks non-stop, gossiping and spreading false information to everyone. When balanced, one is able to speak without any thoughts, feelings, or judgment holding one back. They are healthy both mentally and psychologically. Physically, the throat chakra is responsible for the growth and development of the human body, especially the vocal cords, nose, mouth, jaws teeth, and throat. Emotionally, this chakra revolves around self-expression, whether it is through music, writing, or crafting. When balanced, one is able to accept everything that happens around you especially any difficulties or problems that life throws their way.

When imbalanced, you will have difficulty expressing what it is that you feel and you will often find yourself feeling isolated and shy. Physically, this chakra causes problems for the metabolic system, the thyroid gland, the endocrine system, and the hormones within the body.

It also causes many diseases such as laryngitis, autoimmune thyroiditis, chronic throat defects, hypothyroidism, and many others. When the throat chakra is imbalanced on the emotional level, one will suffer with feelings of restriction, isolation, poor self-esteem, and feel as if no one is listening.

In order to open this chakra, you can sing any song that you desire or hum a tune. Since singing is a way of speaking, it cleanses your throat chakra and makes you able to speak more. It also lifts up your mood. Since this chakra is associated with blue, drinking plenty of water can help the crystals and positive energy to open the chakra point. Speaking is also a way of opening the chakra and saying affirmations can not only help the mind but the throat chakra too. Affirmations are words that make one believe and become whatever they wish to be.

Here are a few throat chakra affirmations that can help unblock and cleanse this chakra:

'I am able to speak freely'
'I am able to speak the truth'
'Everyone listens to what I have to say'
'I am not scared to speak up'
'I am honest with myself and everyone surrounding me'

Crystals for the throat chakra:

Lapis Lazuli is a blue or bluish-white colored marble crystal that works by balancing and healing the throat chakra. Wearing it as a necklace or earrings can not only benefit the throat chakra but the third-eye chakra too.

Amazonite is a green or bluish-green stone that is able to heal the throat chakra, the vibrations are very smooth and relaxing and provide just the right pace for the throat chakra to open.

Moonstones work to activate the throat chakra as well as cleansing and healing all of the other chakras. This is one of the few stones that can be used for any of your chakras.

Iridescent labradorite crystals, especially the dark blue one, can be used to heal the throat chakra as well as increase the energy with the surrounding crystals if not used alone. It can also be used as a necklace or earrings to help keep the vibrations of the throat chakra high.

Aquamarine crystal provides a sort of soothing and cooling healing vibrations that work well with the throat chakra. However, this crystal may be a bit overwhelming the first couple of times one uses it, so make sure you start around five to ten minutes before gradually increasing the time with more practice.

Crystal healing for the throat chakra:

1) Begin by getting comfortable laying down, since you will be placing a crystal on your throat, it is recommended that you lay down. If you sit up then you will be distracted by your tired hands holding the crystal against your throat. If you have a specific crystal necklace then you may use it.

2) Close your eyes and take deep breaths. Feel the way fresh air enters your throat and fills up within the lungs before letting go and exhaling all the negative energy collected within your body. Continue on focusing on your breathing in order to clear your mind and direct attention on your throat.

3) When you feel as if you are calm and ready to carry on with your healing process, bring your attention to the crystal on your throat. Focus on the crystal and visualize a bright light blue glow coming from the crystal. It is spreading and spreading before falling into your throat region. Imagine a warmth filling your neck and extending all the way to your heart before moving upwards to the neck and further up to the mind. Imagine both the heart and the mind feeling open and free, with nothing tying it down.

4) As you visualize the energy flowing through your upper body, think about yourself being able to talk freely and becoming more open with those around you. Visualize yourself having a perfect and free conversation with a friend or family member, when constantly visualize what you want to do, it will seem less scary when you actually do it. This is because

your mind becomes used to the situation although it is all in your head, one of the mind's main weaknesses is that it can't differentiate between what is real and what isn't.

5) Meditate for at least ten to fifteen minutes with the gemstone on your neck. After the healing session, you may want to buy a throat chakra crystal necklace, choker, or earrings that can be used to keep the healing energy within your body.

Chapter 6: Crystal Healing for The Third Eye Chakra

The sixth chakra is the third eye chakra which is where the rational, logical, and critical thinking is rejected, and the concept of psychic ability, seeing into the future, and strong intuition emerges. It is also known as Ajna which signifies to "beyond wisdom". However, just like the translation of Ajna says, the third eye is completely beyond what the human five senses can notice. In fact, the third eye is often known as the sixth sense of the human body, that not a lot of people can achieve. There are many yoga poses that can aid overall to open any of the chakra points, but specific yoga poses for awakening the third eye chakra are known to be very beneficial. The first one is the eagle pose and the child pose. Exercising and eating well-balanced foods can help clear out any negative energies within one's body and it can aid in the process of opening any chakra point. Consuming foods with high omega-3 fats such as walnuts, salmon, sardines, and chia seeds can help enhance the cognitive function as well as opening the third eye chakra.

It is associated with intuition, inner wisdom, and psychic abilities. It is located in the middle of your forehead. The third eye is a complex chakra, it revolves around psychic awakening and abilities. A healthy third eye is able to open your own eyes to see into what the heart really wants, it can also be used to see into what other people desire. This chakra also controls the five senses and can even magnify their power, enabling communication with other planes.

When balanced, communication with other beings such as spirits, angels, and higher beings becomes easier. One is also able to develop gifts such as seeing into the future and strong intuition. One also becomes confident and trusts themselves fully to make the right decision in their life path. Physically, the body is healthy and everything within is in balance with each other. The flow of energy flows and resigns in every part of the body equally and not giving energy to any specific parts while leaving others unattended. In specifics, body parts such as eyes, ears, pineal gland, nose, and even the skeletal system are able to function perfectly. The emotional state of a being is well in balance with the other states when this chakra is open. It grants the ability to choose the way a person lives their life freely through clear thinking and decision making, enhances intuition, awareness, stable mindset, spiritual gifts, as well as seeing past lies.

When imbalanced, one will always doubt their existence which won't help them find their inner happiness and joy. Physically, the third eye is responsible for the hormones imbalance, emotional imbalance, endocrine system that affects one's maturation, metabolism, and growth. Emotionally, an imbalanced third eye chakra can damage the sleep cycle, shift the understanding of reality, cause anxiety, and weakness and fatigue in the body.

Crystals for the third eye chakra:

Lapis Lazuli can help balance and heal the third eye chakra. With its marbled blue color, it is able to bring inner peace to the mind, body, and soul as well as stop negative thoughts.

Amethyst is another stone that can be used to heal this chakra. It can open and cleanse the region, balancing it quickly as well as eliminating negative energy and replacing it with positivity. When working on this chakra, you may use amethyst earring which when worn are the closest to the third eye chakra and are able to keep the healing energy working and circulating all day long. Sodalite is also a very beneficial stone for the third eye chakra since it contains high levels of salt which can be used to cleanse and get rid of any negative energy. It can be used to cleanse, and open the third eye by getting rid of toxins and negativity that might be standing in its way from activation. It can also help one think more logically and clearly as it opens more space to positive emotions and inner peace. Labradorite has very powerful energy which is why if used, one should be cautious. It is an energizing stone which stimulates the flow of energy within the third eye region. This will help to open and clean that area. You may also place this stone under your pillow in order for the healing energies to continue healing your third eye even when you are deep in sleep.

Crystal healing for the third eye chakra:

1) Begin by picking a quiet area with no distractions, awakening this chakra requires a lot of visualization,

energy, and concentration. Make sure your phone is on silent and your doors are locked. Lie down in a comfortable position, place a pillow under your head for the most comfort.

2) Begin the breathing exercise. Breathe in through your nose and exhale through your mouth. Imagine with every exhale, your body becomes more and more relaxed. Focus on how heavy your body feels, almost like the ground is trying to pull you in. Focus on your breathing and don't let your mind and concentration drift away.

3) Place the crystal or crystals on your forehead. You should place one right in the middle of the forehead if you choose to use more than one then make sure they are placed around on the forehead the main crystal in the middle.

4) Bring your attention to the crystals on your forehead. Visualize a bright dark blue light radiating from the crystals and entering your third eye. Make an intention of wishing for your third eye chakra to clear, and open. Welcome any positive thoughts to get rid of the negativity. Continue breathing deeply and with

each exhale, imagine every negative feeling, past bad memories, or childhood traumas simply leaving through your breath. Work on letting go of any discomfort or tension.

5) Visualize healing in your third eye through the crystals. Set an intention for the crystals to work and heal all of your worries and problems. If you wish to awaken your psychic abilities then set an intention for that.

6) Continue for about fifteen minutes once every day. The third eye chakra is very hard to keep open continuously which is why doing it every day with consistency, it will help the body to get used to how the third eye feels being open and naturally align and leave the chakra open. Once the chakra has fully awakened, you may continue performing the crystal healing every other day.

Chapter 7: Crystal Healing for The Crown Chakra

Lastly, the seventh chakra is your crown chakra, also known as Sahasrara which suggests 'thousand-petaled'. The crown chakra is your subconscious chakra, out of all the chakras, this one is very hard to explain and open. It signifies the color purple which is associated with extrasensory perception, intuition, and inner wisdom.

This chakra is the seventh and last chakra, known as the crown chakra. It is also the most difficult chakra to awaken, right before the third eye chakra. It is associated with spirituality, faith, and the Higher Power. This chakra is located at the very top of your head and it is responsible for bringing and attracting things into one's life. High vibrations activate the crown chakra and attract other high vibrational things into one's life. It also represents a connection between and with the Higher Power, the Universe, and yourself.

When balanced, you feel as if everything in your life is going by smoothly and perfectly, there is absolutely no worries or problems. Even if there are, you are able to deal with it on a positive level that it doesn't even affect you mentally, emotionally, physically, or spiritually. You also feel as if something or someone is keeping their eye on you, looking after you, and making sure you live your life the way you want to. Physically, this chakra is responsible for the body's other chakras, when balanced it can influence and make the other chakras more open and healthy. All chakras have the power to influence each other, they are connected. When the crown chakra is open, emotionally one will feel connected with themselves and the world around them.

When the crown chakra is imbalanced, everything in your life seems to go wrong. This is because the crown chakra can also strongly influence the other chakras, making them balanced or imbalanced. Physically, the body can experience trouble in different systems, glands, and organs like the brain, pituitary gland, and the nervous system. One will also start to lack the energy that is required for their everyday life. Illnesses such as amnesia, cognitive delusions, brain tumors, and migraines are caused by the crown chakra. Emotionally, one is filled with feelings of loneliness, lack of connection, depression, and the feeling of insignificance. The feelings of stress, anxiety, depression, hysteria, and other mental illnesses are all the causes of the crown chakra due to its location.

Drinking many herbal teas can help reduce blockage within the crown chakra by cleansing and clearing the toxins out of the body. Consuming purple foods, such as grapes or eggplants can help the chakra to open. Below are some powerful affirmations that can help you.

Since the crown chakra is quite hard to open, affirmations can help the subconscious mind hear what is being said, and open the crown chakra for you since the mind can't tell between what is real and what isn't.

'Today I am open to divine guidance'
'I am love, I am light and I am joy'
'I am connected to my higher self'
'I am one with the universe'
'I have a high vibration'

Crystals for the crown chakra

Clear Quartz is known to be an excellent healing stone for the crown chakra. It works quickly when it comes to cleansing and balancing the crown chakra area. It is also used to stabilize and align the other six chakras after the crown chakra has been awakened. It lets the energy flow in a downward motion, healing the chakras in the process.

Moonstone is also capable of healing the crown chakra by sending its smooth and peaceful vibrations to awaken and cleanse the area. It also has a strong power to help balance other chakras.

Black tourmaline can be used as a grounding stone before proceeding with healing the crown chakra, it can help the effectiveness and rate in which the crown chakra opens increase.

Crystal healing for the crown chakra

1) Sit in a comfortable position, you will be placing your crystal at the top of your head so make sure that your head is tall and your spine is straight. You may

place the crystal on top of your head before starting the breathing exercise. Form your hands into a mudra position, which looks similar to an okay-hand sign.

2) Begin by breathing deeply, inhale and hold the breath for at least three seconds. When exhaling through your mouth, pull the breath for another three-second. Continue to breathe deeply, focus on the way your chest expands and falls with every breath that you take. Visualize your body releasing its toxins, and awakening its energy.

3) After about two to three minutes of breathing, bring your attention to the crystal on top of your head. Feel the weight and pressure it has over you, try to focus on feeling the vibration of the crystal. Once you bring your full attention on the crystal without your mind drifting away, visualize a bright and purple light emerging from the crystal as it surrounds it and your head. Let that light flow there for a minute before being absorbed and pulled by the crown chakra.

4) Proceed by visualizing the light exploring all the different areas within the mind and the crown chakra

region. Imagine every ounce of negativity simply leaving the body and evaporating. Allow yourself to feel lifted as if a big burden or feeling that was holding you back simply leave your body.

5) Become open to the energy and let it explore the crown chakra, healing it and activating it. The crown chakra then activates the flow of energy within the body and is able to travel to any part that requires healing. If you have a specific spot in mind that you wish to heal then direct your attention there. Imagine all the energy flowing into that specific area, cleansing it, and healing it. Visualize yourself being healthy and free.

6) Once you feel as if you have finished, bring your attention and energy back to the crown chakra area on top of your head. Let the energy rest in that area for another minute before closing off the healing session.

7) Overall this healing session should be around ten to fifteen minutes. If you feel awfully tired or not well after the session, then reduce the time. You can raise it again the more your body gets used to the healing.

Make sure to keep a crown chakra stone under your pillow or wear earrings with that stone, this way the crown chakra healing energy will be able to properly stay within the region and keep it open and clear for longer.

Chapter 8: Reiki for The Root Chakra

The root chakra is responsible for providing emotional security and safety in terms of a person's day-to-day activities and survival needs. It is located at the bottom of your spine, where your tailbone is. A balanced root chakra provides a person with calmness and peace relating to your life, but when it is out of balance, you experience feelings of stress and anxiety every single day. The root chakra is all about grounding oneself and being able to feel safe through life.

Physically, the root chakra is responsible for the function of the bladder, legs, kidney, spine, and feet. Keeping this chakra in balance can control the major nerve systems and keep you healthy and nourished. An imbalanced root chakra can make one feel tired all the time and experience lower back pain, hemorrhoids, diarrhea, constipation, sleep disorders, arthritis, and weight issues.

Emotionally, a balanced root chakra can make you feel more relaxed and safe in your everyday environment, thus removing any feelings of anxiety. Problems and conflicts always make us feel scared and anxious, which is not the right way to handle a problem. A balanced root chakra can aid to create a perfect, constructive, and calm mind so when a stressful problem comes up, you will not feel stressed or anxious about that issue. Being able to deal with conflicts smoothly will not make you feel insecure, scared, or angry at what is happening, which is what a blocked root chakra is best known for.

Below is the easiest technique to open your root chakra using Reiki healing with step-by-step guidance. When opening your root chakra, everyone who practices Reiki and uses it for opening chakras has their techniques and below is one of the most efficient ones.

1. Begin by lying down, not sitting. Since the root chakra relates to the spine, you must be comfortable and relaxed. Do not cross your arms or legs, simply lay down in a straight and comfortable position. Make sure the palms of your hands are facing up.

2. Begin to breathe deeply, inhale and hold the breath for three seconds before exhaling it for three seconds. When breathing in and out, do not breathe through your stomach, use your chest instead. When using the chest, the spine moves along with the breathing. This will help the body to relax its muscles and spine. Make an intention to use Reiki, call out to the universe for guidance through your healing process.

3. Focus on your breath and do not let your mind slip away. Begin to resurface the Reiki energy. Visualize your body glowing white and center that the flow of energy on your palms. Imagine it all flowing to your hands. Let yourself feel any tingling sensations or warmth. Lift your hands up and place them down on your lower abdomen. Imagine the light changing color to red as it enters through the lower abdomen to the root chakra. Red is associated with the root chakra and using this color can help open the chakra further.

4. Visualize that red light enters your chakra point and the healing energy that is being sent with it.

You might feel some tingling sensations or warmth down your spine or throughout your body; this indicates that your chakra is being cleared.

5. When you are done, thank the universe for guiding you and for helping you heal yourself. Take some time to relax after the healing process; do not push yourself to do anything. Stay at home, relax, take a hot bath, and let your body heal itself.

Chapter 9: Reiki for The Sacral Chakra

The sacral chakra is the second chakra, which is located in your lower abdomen, usually about one to two inches below the navel. This chakra deals with feelings of sexuality, emotions, and passion. When this chakra is open, your emotions are in balance; you are not overactive or too emotional. Instead, you are filled with passion and a love for your life. However, when this chakra is off-balance, so are your emotions. You lash out often and have problems in your reproductive system.

Physically, the sacral chakra is associated with your sexual organs, the kidneys, and the reproductive system such as testes, ovaries, and the bladder. It is responsible for making sure the hormones and organs function properly as well as the urinary tract and the administration of the circulatory and lymphatic system. Since this chakra deals with releasing and purifying the reproductive system, an open sacral chakra can properly remove toxins from within the body without causing any pain or discomfort. This chakra is associated with the uterus in women and the spleen in men. An imbalance can cause urinary problems, lower back pain, prostate problems, kidney stones, and gynecological problems.

This chakra is the home of your emotions; it is responsible for your happiness, creativity, self-love, and healthy relationships. When in balance, you are comfortable with expressing your emotions rather than feeling like you are being suppressed by other people. You also have no issues regarding your sexuality. When imbalanced, you become helpless, weak, and shy.

1. Begin by getting comfortable, laying down or sitting up. If you lay down, make sure to place a pillow under your head, and another pillow, rolled-up preferably, under your knees to support your legs. Keep your hands on your sides, with palms facing upwards.

2. Close your eyes and take a deep breath in. Hold it for a couple of seconds before letting go. Relax your body and mind as best as you can.

3. Call out to the universe and ask to resurface the Reiki energy from within you. Feel the flow of energy throughout your body as it constantly moves and tries its best to heal you physically, emotionally, and spiritually. Form a Gassho with your hands and place them in front of you where your heart is. Focus on centering the Reiki into your hands as you ask for guidance and healing from the Universe.

4. If your purpose for healing the Sacral chakra is to heal your mind, then feel free to use the Mental/Emotional symbol, Sei He Ki (Say-Hay-Key). Repeat the name three times and begin to visualize the symbol for about a minute.

5. Once you have gathered energy white and pure energy within your hands, proceed by pressing them down onto your sacrum, the lower abdomen a couple of inches below the belly button. This is where the Sacral chakra resides. Visualize sending the Reiki healing onto that chakra; imagine opening it and balancing your emotions. Think of all the negative energy simply letting go and moving on. Replace those

negative feelings that are letting themselves leave your body with those of happiness by thinking back to your happiest memories or about things that make you happy. This will let the body experience its 'true' and happy state.

6. Clear this area for about two to three minutes before placing your hands on your back if you are sitting up or turning to lie on your stomach if you are laying down. Proceed to repeat the following steps. Visualize cleansing and purifying the mind by healing and opening the Sacral chakra. Hold your hands there for two to three minutes.

7. You can also gently massage the area to promote relaxation and letting go of any tension. If you choose to massage the area, then make sure you do it clockwise for women and anticlockwise for men or whichever way feels right to you.

8. When you have finished, thank the Universe for guidance, the Reiki energy for healing, and the

Mental/Emotional symbol for healing your emotions.

Chapter 10: Reiki for The Solar Plexus Chakra

The solar plexus is the third chakra, located in your upper abdomen, a few inches above the belly button. This chakra is responsible for your raw emotions such as anger, intuition, and frustration. The solar plexus ensures that one always expresses their feelings and can deal with problems that arise in their life. When this chakra is balanced, you are calm, confident, self-respectful, and cheerful. But when this chakra is off balance, you find yourself depressed, isolated, in doubt, and frustrated.

Physically, this chakra is responsible for the stomach, nervous system, pancreas, gallbladder, liver, large intestine, eyes, muscular system, and the digestive system. The solar plexus is also responsible for the cellular respiration within the body; it also has control over every organ and system and provides fuel for the body. This chakra is very important since it assists the flow of Ki. When this chakra is blocked, the flow of Ki is weakened and oftentimes blocked from different parts within the body. Issues and problems relating to diabetes, digestive system, hypoglycemia, and arthritis are just some of the many problems that occur due to the imbalance of this chakra.

Emotionally, it also controls the emotions alongside the sacral chakra. If one is experiencing an imbalance mentally and emotionally, this means that it could be either the sacral chakra or any other chakras relating to the emotional state of a person. Oftentimes, when one affects the mind poorly, it affects the other relating chakras. When healing oneself from negativity found within the mind, it is important to open and clear all the chakras relating to the mind. The solar plexus relates to feelings such as cheerfulness, courage, strength, happiness, and motivation. It can also improve the intuitions and gut feelings when balanced properly as well as the manifestation process for one's dreams. When imbalanced, the body experiences anger and frustration quite often in situations that do not require those feelings.

1. When opening this chakra, make sure that you are sitting up for it will be easier to open this chakra. Place your hands on your knees with the palms facing upwards.

2. Since the location of the chakra is on the lower part of your ribs, you will be using your chest to breath. Inhale the air and expand your lungs, hold the breath for at least two to three seconds before exhaling through your mouth. Visualize releasing any negativity through your exhale. Focus on the way your chest rises and falls and do not let your mind wander away. If it does, then gently bring your attention back to your breathing.

3. Just like any other Reiki healing treatments, call on the Universe and ask to heal your solar plexus chakra. Visualize channeling your Reiki and centering it on the palm of your hands.

4. Since this chakra is quite powerful, you will need to use the Power symbol and the Mental/Emotional symbol to help you open and clear this chakra. Repeat the following words three times Choku Rei (Cho-Koo-Ray) and begin to visualize the symbol emerging in your vision. You may also draw the symbol on your palm. Repeat the following words three times Sei He Ki

(Say-Hay-Key), begin to visualize the symbol. You can choose to draw it on the other side of your hands. Either in your vision or physically with a marker.

5. Place your hands on the area above your belly button but below your heart. You will be touching the lower part of your ribs. You should place your hands next to each other and not overlapping each other. Concentrate on making the Reiki energy flow through your hands and to the solar plexus. Visualize it healing the chakra, clearing it of any blockage and releasing the negative emotions through your mouth as you exhale.

6. Use the mantra 'ram'. This specific mantra vibrates the body and helps the negative energies flow out of the chakra. Mantras are just words that are said during meditations, but it can also be used in Reiki practices to ensure that the body is cleared effectively.

7. Once the negative feelings leave, begin to imagine sunflowers or anything yellow. Yellow

stimulates the feelings of joy, and it also represents the solar plexus. Keep your hands on that area for at least two to three minutes before moving on and placing your hands on the other side. If you would like, you can keep cleansing the area for longer than three minutes however long you feel is necessary for your chakra to heal.

8. Place your hands on your back and repeat the same process of visualizing releasing negative energy every time you exhale through your mouth. Think of the symbols to strengthen your intentions and imagine the color yellow to aid you.

9. When done, thank the Universe, Reiki, and the symbols for helping you open your solar plexus chakra.

Chapter 11: Reiki for The Heart Chakra

The heart chakra is located in the heart. It is the center and home of pure love. For the chakra to be balanced, you must be open to give love and receive love to others as well as yourself. It can be hard to accept yourself for who you are, but this is why opening and clearing this chakra through Reiki can make it so much easier. When balanced, the heart chakra gives off love and positivity everywhere within the body, mind, and soul. You immediately feel at peace with yourself and your soul even feels lighter. This chakra can also help when it comes to personal discovery or development. When imbalanced, the heart chakra experiences hate and negative emotions causing the body's function to fail.

Physically, this chakra is responsible for the function of the heart, the circulatory system, thymus gland, breasts, the respiratory system, diaphragm, ribs, hands, arms, and shoulders, in other words, almost everything that surrounds the heart including lungs and blood circulation. The heart chakra is the life force that keeps us alive by beating the muscle, known as a heart, within our body and distributing blood throughout the system. Since this chakra is also associated with the thymus gland, it is responsible for your healthy immune system which requires the T-cells produced by the thymus gland. When imbalanced, the heart chakra is responsible for lung disease, breathing difficulty, breast cancer, high blood pressure, and many other health issues.

Emotionally, the heart chakra is very vulnerable to negative emotions, and it is up to us to balance and open this chakra to live, laugh, and love life. When this chakra is imbalanced, a person experiences the feelings of jealousy, hatred, isolation, fear, grief, betrayal, and loneliness. These feelings also have the power to influence the environment, and they can cause separation, divorce, abandonment, emotional abuse, and other emotional distress events. Negative emotions attract negative situations.
To avoid those feelings, one must open their heart chakra to love and acceptance. Love is the key to helping yourself heal emotionally and mentally if it is depression, negative thinking, or anxiety that you are dealing with.

1. Begin by lying down and relaxing comfortably. Place a pillow under your head, and another under your knees. Leave your hands lying next to your body with the palms facing up. Take a minute to focus and clear your mind by breathing deeply.

2. Proceed by calling on the Reiki energy, asking for guidance, and imagining the Power symbol and saying its name three times, Choku Rei (Cho-Koo-Ray). Place an intention to receive protection from anything negative in your life: negative events, negative emotions, and negative people. This will help you feel safer and at ease from negativity.

3. Channel your Reiki energy and concentrate on centering it on your hands. Allow the flow of white energy to resurface in your palms and glow a white and pure color. Place your hands on your heart, one over the other. Allow the energy to sink into your heart chakra and visualize the white-colored light changing into a bright green associated with the heart chakra.

4. Visualize the color glowing brighter and brighter as it opens your heart chakra to all the love and happiness that you deserve. Think of the people whom you care deeply for. Imagine sending them your love and blessing to ensure that they are safe and happy with their life. Think of different times when love was expressed and given to you, even the small things that made you happy still count!

5. Open yourself to healing within your heart. Use the mantra 'yam' to help you open this chakra further. Spend some time to opening your chakra; do not rush through the process, but let your body heal its heart.

6. When you think you have finished, end the session by thanking the Universe, Reiki, and the Power symbol for helping you. Proceed by doing something that makes you happy or something that you love. Take a warm and relaxing bath, and give yourself some love before you go on giving others love.

Chapter 12: Reiki for The Throat Chakra

The fifth chakra is the throat chakra which is located in your neck and throat region. This chakra is responsible for your communication and release of emotions in your life. It relates to the mouth and ears since it is associated with speaking and hearing. When balanced, one can speak up without a problem and listen to everything another has to say. A person with a balanced throat chakra is healthy mentally and psychologically. You can speak up without a doubt and inspire yourself and others around you. When this chakra is blocked, one finds it hard to express their feelings in terms of words; they become isolated, shy, and keep to themselves.

Physically, this chakra is responsible for the human endocrine system associated with hormones, the thyroid gland, and metabolic system, and it takes care of the trachea, teeth, throat, mouth, larynx, nose, the carotid arteries, and the nose. The throat chakra is responsible for the development and growth of the human body both physically and mentally. It is also responsible for the diseases and physical problems such as autoimmune thyroiditis, laryngitis, hypothyroidism, gum defects, headaches, chronic throat defects, jaw pain, fatigue, lack of motivation, cold sores, obstruction within speech, and a hoarse voice. Many also resort to gossiping, lying, and not saying the truth about themselves and other people around them.

Emotionally, the throat chakra is connected to listening to people, music, and words, writing, self-expression, taste, creativity, and smell. When this chakra is well-balanced, you can speak and listen to people without anything stopping you from it. Your mind can also accept everything that happens to you positively. When the throat chakra is off-balance, then one person experiences feelings of hate, bitterness, feeling as if no one is listening to what they have to say, poor self-esteem, and many dominant feelings like aggression and anger.

1. Begin by sitting up or lying down comfortably with a pillow under the knees, but not under the head. Lay down straight or sit up straight. Make sure your head is not sulking, but nice straight

and tall. Place your hands on your knees or on each side of your body is lying down and make sure the palms are facing upwards.

2. Begin the usual Reiki session by calling out to the Universe and making an intention to help yourself speak up more and become more involved with the community, if that is your goal. You will require the Mental/Emotional symbol, since the inability to speak up comes from the mind and not the physical body, unless one has an issue with the throat. Repeat the words Sei He Ki (Say-Hay-Key) three times before imagining yourself sitting or lying in a room similar to the one you are in right now, but the walls are covered with the Mental/Emotional symbol.

3. While looking at that symbol, focus on resurfacing your Reiki and centering it in your hands. Imagine a white light emerging from within your hands. Lift them up and place them on your collar bone, one hand over the other. Visualize the healing energy of Reiki leaving your hands and sinking deep through your body

and making its way to the center of the throat chakra.

4. Think of yourself being able to talk freely with no doubts or no mental blockages. Imagine everyone wanting to hear what you have to say and the inability of speaking fading away into a positive loud and clear voice.

5. While holding your hands on that area, use the mantra 'ham' which can create vibrations that have the power to alter the flow of energy within the communication center. Once you spend at least two to three minutes healing that part of your body, move your hands upward and extend the healing energy to your throat. Hold your hands there for another brief two to three minutes before rotating and moving them to the back of your neck.

6. Once you feel as if you healed enough of your throat chakra, close the treatment by repeating Choku Rei (Cho-Koo-Ray) to seal the healing energy within you.

7. Thank the Universe for guidance, the Reiki energy for healing, and the symbols for helping. After the treatment, take some time to read out loud to work on your voice since you might be filled with an overwhelming urge to speak and rant about almost anything.

Chapter 13: Reiki for The Third Eye Chakra

The sixth chakra is your third eye chakra that deals with psychic powers, intuition, and intelligence. This chakra is located on your forehead, slightly between your two brows, and it is the origin of your psychic abilities. When this chakra is balanced, one can see the inner and outer worlds beyond the five senses. Many spiritual gifts reside in this chakra such as psychic vision, seeing into the future, and communicating with other beings and spirits. When in balance, you can see what you and other people truly desire. You act confidently and know your exact purpose in life. You have a strong sense when it comes to your inner truth and you trust your intuition to lead you through your life path. When the third eye is imbalanced, you begin to doubt your existence and asking questions about your life purpose or why are you alive. You can't find inner happiness and can't seem to find joy in your life.

Physically, the third eye chakra affects your hormones associated with many different parts within your physical, mental, and emotional aspect. This chakra is also responsible for the endocrine system that looks after one's growth, maturation, tissue function, metabolism, mood, and many other functions. The third eye looks after the ears, eyes, pineal gland, nose, and the skeletal system within one's body. It also controls the five senses, so when the third eye is open and balanced, the five senses are heightened and enables one to communicate with other planes and beings out of what the physical eyes can see.

Emotionally, this chakra grants you the ability to form and perceive your own opinions and beliefs on life, how you live, and what you believe in. It also grants you spiritual gifts, intuition enhancement, personal visions, predictions, seeing past peoples facades, and many others. This chakra is responsible for regulating your growth, sleep cycle, stable mind, clarity, awareness, and aging by being in control of the pineal gland. Balanced third eye chakra can give sharpness in mind, good memory, and good visualization skills. An imbalance can cause a shift in reality and understanding reality–one will rely too much on luck and fate. Worrying too much and anxiety also comes from the imbalance of this chakra.

1. Start by getting comfortable and lying down. Do not place a pillow under your head, only under your knees. You can use a blanket to keep you warm, but make sure to leave your hands by your sides on top of the blanket.

2. Proceed by asking the Universe to open your third eye and make an intention to open it using Reiki. Channel and center your Reiki energy on your hands.

3. Since opening the third eye is one of the most difficult chakra openings, you will need to use the Power symbol and the Mental/Emotional symbol. On the palm of your hand, using a marker draw the symbol Cho Ku Rei (Cho-Koo-Ray) and visualize the symbol activating. On the other side of your hand, draw the symbol Sei He Ki (Say-Hay-Key) and activate it. You will only need to draw the symbol on one of your hands.

4. Place your hand, the one with the symbols, on your third eye which is on your forehead. Place the other hand over the hand with the symbols.

Close your eyes and concentrate on visualizing a white light emerging and entering the third eye, immediately lifting your spirits up. Focus on transmitting the energy and getting rid of any tensions and blockages. Visualize the third eye opening, enhancing your intuition and other psychic abilities. Keep your hands there for two to three minutes before moving on.

5. Remove the hand with no symbol. Using your index finger of the symbol one, place the finger down on the third eye chakra and start to massage it in a clockwise circulation for women and an anticlockwise circulation for male. You can then join in with the mantra 'Ksham' for another two to three minutes.

6. When you feel as if you have finished, proceed by thanking the Universe, Reiki, and the symbols for help.

Chapter 14: Reiki for The Crown Chakra

The crown chakra is the seventh and last chakra which related to spirituality, religion, God, and faith. The crown chakra is located at the very top of your head. It represents the connection to your Higher Self and even acts as a magnet of anything you desire. When this chakra is balanced, you feel a strong connection to the Higher Power and the Universe. This connection is similar to the one of Reiki.

You feel as if someone or something is keeping their eye on you, making sure that everything in your life goes by smoothly.

There are no negative people or problems and difficulties in your life. You live in gratitude and in happiness for everything that you have. You are at a high vibration and attracting only good and positive things to yourself. But when the crown chakra is imbalanced, you are filled with feelings of loneliness and insignificance.

You experience a lack of connection with yourself and the world around you. One is also afraid of one change and what life has to offer.

Physically the crown chakra is responsible for a lot of glands, systems, and organs within the body such as the pituitary gland, the brain, and the nervous system. When balanced, the body is healthy and full of energy. However, when imbalanced, the body suffers from many illnesses relating to strokes, migraines, brain tumors, cognitive delusions, coma, and amnesia.

Emotionally, the crown chakra is the consciousness part of the body. It unites the mind and the body as one and connects to the spirit, Higher Power, the Universe, or God. When this chakra is balanced mentally and emotionally, a person feels stable. When this chakra is off-balanced, there are feelings of anxiety, stress, depression, hysteria, and many other related mental illnesses.

1. Begin by getting comfortable and sitting up. Make sure your spine is long and straight. Place your hands with the palms facing upwards on your knees, close your eyes, and begin to breathe deeply. Inhale through your nose; hold the breath anywhere from two to three seconds before letting go through your mouth. Make sure

when exhaling you drag the breath out for another two to three seconds.

2. Form your hands into a Gassho position. Draw the power of Reiki and ask the Universe for guidance since the crown chakra is the hardest to open. Channel the energy in your hands. Lift your hands up as high as you can while still maintaining the Gassho position.

3. Repeat Choku Rei (Cho-Koo-Ray) three times and make an intention to heighten the power of this Reiki treatment. Begin to visualize the symbol floating in front of you and a bright white light.

4. Visualize the white light within your hands joining together with the white light from the symbol before shooting a beam of light into your crown chakra. Feel the tingling sensations and make an intention to open this chakra. Keep on breathing deeply as you begin to say the mantra 'ohm' to clear your crown chakra.

5. Hold the position for about three minutes before placing your hands on top of your head. Visualize giving more healing energy to the crown chakra and concentrate on opening the crown and healing the mind and body, getting rid of any negative emotions that do not belong within your mind. Proceed to heal for another three minutes.

6. When finished, thank the Universe, Reiki, and the Power symbol for their help. You should take some time off to yourself to rest and let the crown chakra heal itself. Raise your vibrations by doing something that you enjoy and love deeply.

Conclusion

Thank you for making it through to the end of Crystal and Reiki for The Seven Chakras: Discover How to Heal Your Body, Increase Spiritual Energy and Balance Your Chakras with the Power of Crystals and Reiki. Let's hope it was informative and able to provide you with all the tools you need to achieve your goals of healing yourself and increasing your energy with crystals.

The next step is to put everything that you've learned about crystals and how they work to the test. All you need is a crystal, belief, and intentions. Begin by slowly practicing healing around five to ten minutes a day until you get used to the energy and how it works. You wouldn't want to jump into increasing your own energy if your body is unable to get used to the overwhelming power that comes from within. Use the power of Reiki to help yourself, your family, your friends, and others around you. Not only can Reiki heal, but it can also send you on a spiritual journey full of self-discovery and it can push you to your life path.

Lightning Source UK Ltd.
Milton Keynes UK
UKHW02215426102
392885UK00006B/424

9 781803 127538